Improving School Climate

Leadership Techniques
for
Principals

by

Edgar A. Kelley

National Association of Secondary School Principals
Reston, Virginia

About the Author

Edgar A. Kelley is a professor of administration, curriculum and instruction at The University of Nebraska-Lincoln. A former classroom teacher and secondary school principal, he has had a long-standing interest in school climate and its assessment: He has served as a consultant on school climate in a number of settings, including Teacher Corps and for NASSP workshops. Part of the preparation of this monograph was funded by a grant made by Region IV, Phi Delta Kappa.

Contents

Foreword

School climate, an elusive but encompassing component of secondary education, is gaining new recognition today. Not only is it essential to good student achievement but it is important to positive student attitudes. A favorable school climate provides the framework within which students, teachers, administrators, and parents function cooperatively and productively.

A beneficial school climate does not happen by accident. It takes planning and work and leadership. The result, however, is that it pays tangible dividends. It can produce better learning as well as better feelings all around. Building a positive climate, therefore, should have high priority today.

School climate is more than good morale, more than a happy glow. As the author makes clear, a positive climate includes everyone's focusing on school goals and student outcomes as well as on personal relationships and salutory feelings. The ideal school climate engages everyone enthusiastically in achieving the individual and group goals at hand.

A positive school climate is perhaps the single most important expression of educational leadership, as the recent British study *Fifteen Thousand Hours* makes clear. The differences from school to school according to this study center upon the principal's ability to build a supportive, challenging, and positive school climate. Schools can make a difference in the present and future lives of students—and this difference is caused by the quality of climate. An environment of high expectations and generous assistance produces results.

This monograph provides an excellent description of the components of school climate and provides solid advice to school administrators on how to go about building a more vigorous climate. It can be a checklist to monitor present circumstances as well as an agenda for further action. We commend it to your use.

We also wish to express our appreciation to Edgar A. Kelley for this and other important contributions to secondary education and to the continuing work of NASSP on behalf of practitioners.

Scott D. Thomson
Executive Director
NASSP

CHAPTER 1

Introduction

S ome schools are cheerful and hum with excitement and purpose. Others seem to lack enthusiasm. Some classrooms are alive with expectancy. Others appear moribund. Some people who work and study in schools see each new day and each new person as opportunities for improving their understanding of the world around them. Others fear that today will be worse than yesterday. These feelings of satisfaction and productivity constitute school climate.

All human beings exist in a natural environment and in social environments, each one having a climate formed by the conditions present. Judgments about what makes a "good" or a "bad" climate in a social environment are based on how well it meets the expectations of those who live in, work in, are influenced by, or are familiar with that particular environment.

The expectations for social environments can be described by the emphasis given to satisfaction, to productivity, or to both. In some environments, the major purpose is pleasure, or satisfaction; thus, at a birthday party, the major concern is with satisfaction. In other environments, the primary concern is productivity or task accomplishment; thus mouth-to-mouth resuscitation has an ultimate goal of saving a life, and few would suggest that the major concern should be with whether or not the person administering mouth-to-mouth resuscitation finds the activity pleasurable. A third could be those settings in which concern is high for the highest possible levels of both satisfaction and productivity.

Schools are social environments, and educators must attend to the levels of satisfaction and to the levels of productivity which are outcomes of those environments. At any particular time, the most obvious concerns might be with the morale of students, the job satisfaction of staff members, or the extent to which parents and patrons approve of the school and its programs. These concerns do not mean that there is little concern about student performance, falling test scores, or teacher performance. There can be a simultaneous concern for development or maintenance of self-esteem and self-reliance on the part of the students and staff. An environment in which people are happy to study and to work is important.

A Definition of School Climate

The climate of a social environment is formed by the norms, beliefs, and attitudes reflected in the conditions, events, and practices of a particular environment. In this context, climate refers to prevailing or normative conditions which are relatively enduring over time and which can be used to distinguish one environment from another. Climate conditions, as perceived by persons who work within or know a particular environment, serve as the basis for establishing expectations and interpreting events or activities which occur within that environment.

Any single environment may have patterns, practices, and conditions which enhance the attainment of satisfaction and accomplishment while also having other patterns, practices, and conditions which impede the attainment of satisfaction and productivity.

Changes in conditions, events, and practices can and often do occur prior to any changes in norms, beliefs and attitudes; but success in changing the climate of an environment usually requires change at both the attitudinal and behavioral levels. Changes which are made within an environment may lead to increased, decreased, or unchanged levels of either or both satisfaction and productivity.

Because individuals and groups differ in their values and perceptions of what is valuable and meaningful, they also differ in their descriptions of what climate conditions or outcomes are most important. Consequently, one of the first steps in organizing for assessment of climate outcomes or in planning for improvement of the climate in a school environment is to identify the expectations of those people who have a legitimate interest in the conditions which exist and the outcomes which occur.

Although there are differences between school environments, the following assumptions form the philosophical viewpoint expressed in this monograph:

- The education of youth is important.

- The ultimate criterion for assessment of the quality of school environments is concern with the levels of productivity and satisfaction attained by students.

- Learning is both a social and a psychological process.

- Individuals, in any role or position, act according to the expectations which others hold for their behavior.

- Differences between schools in the characteristics of schools as social institutions is the primary determinant of differences in outcomes attained by students. These differences are more important than aptitude of the student or socioeconomic status of the home. (Rutter, et al., 1979.)

- When student outcomes or achievement are the focal point of climate assessment or development, the most appropriate unit for data analysis is the classroom. Analysis of data by classroom rather than by school building accounts for an average of 40 percent of the variation in the levels of student achievement attained in differing educational environments. (Madaus, et al., 1979.)

- Schools which attain high levels of student outcomes have faculties who: (a) accept the basic objectives of the school; (b) have a strong commitment to high expectations for students and for student achievement; and (c) accept responsibility for achieving stated goals. By contrast, schools with low or declining levels of student achievement are characterized by "complacency and acceptance of things as they are; no one 'rocks the boat,' and there is an apparent unwillingness to attend to problems which might upset the calm or the good staff relations." (Brookover and Lezotte, 1977.)

- Strong leadership by the principal is an important factor in improving school climate when the desired outcome is improvement in student attainment of learning outcomes. (Brookover and Lezotte, 1977; Lezotte, et al., 1980.)

- "Effective schools have a common belief that all students can learn, and they have adopted an instructional orientation that reflects this belief." (Lezotte, et al., 1980.)

Taken collectively, these assumptions form the basis for the central theme of this monograph: *schools can make a difference in what happens to the people who work and study in school environments.*

CHAPTER 2

Climate Assessment in Schools

Careful assessment of classroom or school climate should precede the adoption and implementation of plans for the improvement of those environments. Unfortunately, it is not uncommon to see practices adopted and innovations implemented with little or no formal assessment of the current state of the environments (Lezotte, et al., 1980).

Climate assessment, and methods and tools selected for the assessment of climate, should proceed from the selection of an operating definition of climate which is validated for, and applied to, a specific environment. The definition of climate should reflect assumptions made about the importance of satisfaction as an outcome, the importance of productivity as an outcome, and the relationship which exists between satisfaction and productivity, i.e., does increased satisfaction lead to increased productivity? The assumptions can be based on findings of past research studies, on beliefs which are present in the environment, or a mixture of facts and beliefs.

Studies of Morale

One finding of the Western Electric studies was that the function of any organization is twofold: "producing a product and . . . creating and distributing satisfactions

5

among the individual members of the organization." This stimulated a number of studies based on the assumption that a direct and causal link between human satisfaction and human productivity exists. When this assumption is the starting point for the creation or adoption of a definition of climate, climate and morale are being used as synonymous terms.

Since the 1950s, the research literature has consistently reported that the relationship between satisfaction and productivity is neither predictive nor causal. This lack of a predictive link between satisfaction (morale) and performance or productivity led most theorists and researchers to conclude by the 1960s that morale studies are important if measures of satisfaction are sought, but are relatively meaningless for use in making inferences about productivity. Thus, *morale* and *climate* are related but conceptually distinct terms.

According to Lezotte and others (1980): "The most commonly held notion of climate is the *organizational* climate or social climate in which the emphasis is on the affective, satisfaction-based adult relationships." Thus, a concern for staff morale in school settings is often accompanied by an assumption that this will lead to increased productivity by staff and to increased satisfaction and achievement by students. This linkage remains unproven (Lezotte, et al., 1980; Walberg, 1979; ERIC, 1978).

Despite research evidence which is neutral or contradictory, most practicing educators have continued to use "morale" and "climate" as synonymous or analagous terms. If this definition is accepted in a particular setting, two useful sources are *School Climate Improvement: A Challenge to the School Administrator,* published by Phi Delta Kappa, and *School Climate: Evaluation and Implementation,* published by CADRE.

Climate Studies

Although the use of the term *climate* (as a label for a concern with both productivity and satisfaction as well as the relationships which exist between these two dimensions) does not appear in the research literature until the mid-1950s, the development of climate as a concept separate from morale is based on the work of H. A. Murray during the 1930s. Murray described behavior as "a function of the relationship between the person and his environment." Both the person and the environment have needs or expectations; Murray described this relationship as being that which exists between the "needs" of the individual and the "press" (organizational needs and expectations) of the environment.

Two efforts at the development of valid and reliable assessment tools for the measure of climate in school environments include the work of George Stern and others at the Psychological Research Center at Syracuse University (Stern, 1970) and the work of Rudolf H. Moos and others at the Social Ecology Laboratory at Stanford University (Moos, 1974; Consulting Psychologists Press, 1979). Both Stern and Moos have based their work on concepts derived from Murray.

In addition to the work of Murray, Stern and Moos, a number of other research efforts that explore both satisfaction and productivity are summarized in Walberg (1979) and Lezotte, et al. (1980).

Assessment Tools

The number and variety of tools available for assessment of climate as perceived by staff or students is extensive. Care should be taken to select those tools that provide information which is desired and usable for planning and decision making. Criteria for selection of tools include:

- Congruence or compatibility with the definition of climate established for the environment being measured.

- Acceptable levels of reliability and validity for tools selected.

- Feasibility of tools and procedures selected, including ease of administration, reasonable costs for administration, and availability of expertise for interpretation of data.

In February, 1978, the ERIC Clearinghouse on Educational Management issued a *Research Action Brief* on school climate. Noting that practicing educators and administrators tend to view school climate in terms different from those used by researchers, it reviewed two approaches to the assessment of school climate: the Organizational Climate Description Questionnaire (OCDQ) and the School District Climate Profile (SDCP). These two along with the "Syracuse Indexes" (developed by George Stern and his associates) and the "Social Climate Scales" (developed by Rudolf H. Moos and his associates) are four examples of assessment tools.

OCDQ. This tool, widely used by both researchers and practitioners, is designed to measure faculty perceptions of school climate. It consists of 64 items organized in eight categories: four (disengagement, hindrance, esprit, and intimacy) measure the characteristics of the faculty as a group; the other four (aloofness, production emphasis, thrust, and consideration) measure the faculty perceptions of the principal as a leader.

Halpin and Croft, the creators of the OCDQ, found that the two categories with the most meaning were *esprit* (teacher morale) and *thrust* (extent to which the principal motivates teachers by setting a good example and by moving the organization toward attainment of desired goals). Findings from their research efforts led to the description of schools as having "open" or "closed" climates.

While its widespread use provides a basis for comparison of OCDQ scores with other settings, the OCDQ has a number of limitations when compared to other approaches for measurement of school climate. It is, primarily, a morale instrument. In addition, as Owens (1970) reported, the OCDQ was designed for use in elementary schools and "is apparently not well suited to large, urban, or secondary schools, and whether it can appropriately be used for evaluating a school's effectiveness—a possibility which Halpin has raised—remains very much in question."

THE SCHOOL DISTRICT CLIMATE PROFILE (SDCP). The SDCP is a questionnaire to measure satisfaction with current conditions and processes in school environments. Questions are organized into four broad categories: general climate factors, program determinants, process determinants, and material determinants. They are designed to obtain perceptions about the quality of leadership styles, problem-solving and decision-making methods, conflict resolution, interpersonal relations, goal setting, organizational communication, administrator and staff preparation, and so forth. Used as a needs assessment tool, with audiences responding on a scale from "ideal" to "real," the SCDP is useful for identifying target areas for climate improvement projects.

As a measure of climate, however, it must be questioned. The SDCP measures morale. Research does not indicate whether or not the four categories can be accepted as valid representations of climate. Levels of instrument reliability, validity, and concurrent or predictive validity with other measures have not been adequately researched and reported.

Perhaps the greatest weakness of the SDCP is "its conceptual vagueness," a point noted in the ERIC (1978) review of this instrument. One example of the conceptual vagueness of the SDCP is its assumption that open climates are inherently better than closed climates and that increases in satisfaction will be invariably accompanied by increases in achievement or productivity. The developers and the disseminators of the SDCP do not provide evidence to support the assumption; and other research evidence, discussed elsewhere in this monograph, does not lend support to these assumptions.

THE SYRACUSE INDEXES. Research and development of several measurement devices designed to check people's perceptions about the impact of various environments on satisfaction and productivity have been under way at the Psychological Research Center at Syracuse University for more than two decades. Until his death, George Stern directed these efforts. All of the "Syracuse Indexes" are based on the psychological constructs suggested by H. A. Murray. Most have been widely used in a number of settings for both research purposes and as a basis for diagnosis of environments so that climate development plans could be formulated.

Instruments developed and validated include: the Elementary and Secondary School Index (ESI); the High School Characteristics Index (HSCI); the Classroom Environment Index (CEI); the Organizational Climate Index (OCI); the College Characteristics Index (CCI); and the Activities Index (AI).

Four tools are especially appropriate for use in secondary schools:

- *The Organizational Climate Index (OCI).* The OCI measures perceptions of faculty and employees. The original version contained 300 items and provided measures of 30 scales, six first-order factors and two second-order factors. Further refinement has resulted in a short form of the OCI (80 items) which provides measures of six first-order factors and two second-order factors. The first-order factors are (a) intellectual climate, (b) achievement standards, (c) personal dignity, (d) organizational effectiveness, (e) orderliness, and (f) impulse control. These six factors, by further factor analysis and combination, yield two major dimensions of school environments as perceived by staff: *development press* and *task effectiveness.*

- *The High School Characteristics Index (HSCI), the Classroom Environment Index (CEI) and the Elementary and Secondary School Index (ESI).* All three instruments are used to measure student perceptions of climate. The HSCI, developed first, has 300 items and yields information about 30 scales, seven first-order factors and three second-order factors. The CEI, developed for use with classroom populations, is similar in style and output to the HSCI. The ESI is a short form of the HSCI or CEI; it has 61 items and outputs are the first-order and second-order factors. The seven first-order factors include: (a) intellectual climate, (b) expressiveness, (c) group social life, (d) personal dignity, (e) achievement standards, (f) control, and (g) peer group dominance. The identification of second-order factors yields three dimensions. The first dimension, *development press,* is a combination of the first five of the first-order factors. The other two second-order factors, *control* and *peer group dominance,* are identical to their first-order factor counterparts.

The Syracuse Indexes are compatible with definitions of school climate that stress both satisfaction and productivity. In addition, levels of known reliability and validity as well as norms for school populations are available for interpretation of data. Its weaknesses include difficulty in using the instruments for measurement of "real" and "ideal" perceptions, i.e., use for needs assessment purposes, as well as the problems involved in sending data to Syracuse University for scoring and in obtaining expert interpretation of data. Costs of administration, data analysis, and interpretation are likely to be higher than those involved in the use of other assessment approaches but are not necessarily excessive for many schools or school districts.

Further information about the Syracuse Indexes, including sample sets of the instruments and answer sheets, can be obtained from the Center for Instructional Development, Test Scoring and Evaluation Services, 250 Machinery Hall, Syracuse University, Syracuse, N.Y. 13210.

THE SOCIAL CLIMATE SCALES. Rudolf Moos and his associates at the Social Ecology Laboratory at Stanford University have developed 12 instruments, known collectively as the Social Climate Scales. The series is available from Consulting Psychologists Press, Inc., 577 College Avenue, Palo Alto, Calif. 94306.

The 1979 catalog of Consulting Psychologists Press describes these scales as follows:

This . . . series of scales makes it possible to measure the "personalities" of environments, to evaluate the impact of different interventions, to compare the judgments of staff and rank-and-file group members.

Each of these scales consists of 90 or 100 true-false items and yields from 7 to 10 easily-computed scores which cover three major dimensions of a social environment: the nature and intensity of personal relationships; personal growth and self-enhancement influences; and system maintenance and change dimensions. A subscale usually consists of 9 to 10 items selected by internal consistency procedures.

Each scale has also been adapted to measure the ideal social environment (Form I) or the expectations one has of an environment (Form E).

11

Short forms (Form S), requiring only 5 to 10 minutes to complete, yield good reliability coefficients.

The two social climate scales with greatest applicability for school environments are the Work Environment Scale (WES), appropriate for use with faculties, and the Classroom Environment Scale (CES), appropriate for use with secondary school students. The CES measures involvement, affiliation, and teacher support as subscales of the relationship dimension; task orientation and competition as subscales of the personal growth or goal orientation dimension; and, order and organization, rule clarity, teacher control, and innovation as subscales of the system maintenance and change dimension.

The Social Climate Scales meet the criteria for selection of tools and procedures if the accepted definition of climate stresses both productivity and satisfaction. In addition, the availability of parallel forms to measure the "real," "ideal," and "expected" environment permits the use of needs assessment procedures to identify and target climate development activities.

OTHER MEASURES OF CLIMATE. A number of other instruments and approaches have been used for the measurement of school climate. Two books provide excellent reviews of research findings and of tools or procedures for assessment: *Educational Environments and Effects* (Walberg, 1979) and *School Learning Climate and Student Achievement* (Lezotte, et al., 1980).

One climate instrument widely used in the United States, England, Australia, and Canada is the Learning Environment Inventory (LEI), which is an outgrowth of the older Classroom Climate Questionnaire (CCQ). The LEI is used with secondary school students to measure such school characteristics as: cohesiveness, diversity, formality, speed, environment, friction, goal direction, favoritism, difficulty, apathy, democracy, cliquishness, satisfaction, disorganization, and competitiveness. A shorter variation of the LEI is the "My Class" or "My School" form to be used with elementary school students.

Still another tool available is the Quality of School Life (QSL) instrument (Epstein and McPartland, 1978). It has 27 items that measure three dimensions: students' satisfaction with school, commitment to classwork, and reactions to teachers.

Using Existing Data To Assess Climate

Assessors of the climate of a classroom or school can often use data already available. In fact, such data can often be more useful than the data collected with other tools. Schools have an abundance of data which can be organized to pinpoint areas of strength and areas for environmental change. Examples of such data include scores on aptitude tests and achievement tests, information on absenteeism, tardiness, levels of student involvement, disciplinary referrals, and academic achievement.

If existing information is used, two steps should be followed to plan and organize data: First, select the types of comparisons to be made to determine the meaning of data; second, adopt simple plans for organizing data to show patterns occurring over extended periods of time.

STANDARDS FOR COMPARISON OF DATA. A number of possible bases of comparison can be used to interpret data already present in the school environment. One method is to compare data for the current school year with earlier data. A second method is to compare data from one environment with data from comparable environments, for example, attendance data for one school with attendance data from similar schools. A third approach to organizing data is to compare data from an environment with normative data from a district, state, or region. Yet another method is to establish standards for determining whether or not data are to be judged as acceptable or as being areas in which efforts to improve should be made; for example, theory-based approaches would suggest that if 80 percent of a group find an outcome to be present within an environment and acceptable then it may be unnecessary or undesirable to seek change.

ORGANIZING DATA. Regardless of the standard or standards selected for comparison with existing data, plans should be made to organize and report the data. Charts that show data for a single dimension over an extended period of time can be helpful in communicating to all interested audiences how well the school is doing. A well-designed chart can summarize data from several years and can be placed on a single page. Selected "barometers" of school performance can be painted on the walls of the school or in other locations where students, patrons, and staff are reminded of what the school is accomplishing. Examples of such charts might include:

- A chart of average daily attendance for the past five years with comparisons to similar school environments or to other standards as selected in the environment.

- A chart of academic achievement for the past five years. This might be average grade point averages for students in the school. Another approach would be to show achievement test data for the student population in comparison to aptitude test data—such a chart could be developed to demonstrate relationship between aptitude and achievement without comparison to other schools or to normative data, for example, the aptitude line could be a straight line in the middle of the chart with the achievement test data plotted against the aptitude data to show the extent to which the student population performed worse than or better than the levels which would be predicted by aptitude test data.

- A chart showing average student involvement in in-school and out-of-school activities, including work, can be informative about student interests and development.

Summary

A few of the tools and procedures available for climate assessment have been reviewed and discussed in this chapter. Practices which are selected for use, however, should give consideration to a clear definition of climate, to the selection of tools and procedures which are compatible with that definition, and should seek to use and organize existing data as a means of diagnosing how well the school or classroom environment is meeting goals of both satisfaction (morale) and productivity (achievement).

CHAPTER 3

Planning for Climate Development

P lanning for climate development is essential. In fact, it is often better to do nothing than to proceed without careful planning.

In any social environment the perceived "leader," by virtue of ascribed or earned role, is the major determiner of the climate. Thus, a teacher's actions will be the single most important determinant of the climate in a classroom. Likewise, the principal has a comparable role in influencing the overall climate in the school building. At the district level, central office administrators can and do have a major role in setting and fulfilling the conditions which enhance or impede the development of positive building and classroom climates.

Although educational researchers and practitioners don't always agree on how to solve specific problems, they do agree that some school climates are good and some are bad and that efforts to assess and improve school climate are important. (ERIC, 1978.)

One problem, common to many individuals and in many settings, is the attempt to describe optimum environments, i.e., a "perfect" environment composed of conditions and processes appropriate for every institutional setting. Much of the literature read by practitioners concerned about climate development falls into this trap. As one writer observed, "The concept of a single optimum environment is for the human animal, not the human being; it is a 'zoo view' of humanity that precludes human dignity'' (Ewald, 1967).

But what is the alternative to the "zoo view"? The alternative is diagnosis of environmental conditions and environmental outcomes, and the relationships between the two, so that it is possible to select, construct, adjust, or modify environmental conditions in ways which lead to increased productivity and satisfaction for human beings who act within those environments.

No particular characteristic, activity, or behavior has inherent value for all settings; indeed, the worth of any tool or strategy must be determined in each environment. The most common error of practitioners, however, is their effort to identify methods or tools which will be "best" when applied to any or all situations.

A related problem is the selection of a single tool or strategy for use with all persons in a particular setting. Examples include the selection of instructional materials, practices used in grouping students for instruction, practices used for guidance and counseling, the selection of instructional methods, practices used for student discipline, and practices used for teacher supervision.

In the plan suggested in this chapter for use in planning climate improvement, persons responsible for planning are encouraged to: (a) identify real concerns and needs, (b) involve legitimate audiences, both internal and external to the school, in planning and affirming plans, and (c) to focus on maintenance or improvement of desired outcomes rather than on advocacy of any particular methodology or strategy.

Figure 1 outlines a step-by-step approach that can be used in the planning of climate assessment or development projects. Each step is described briefly in the paragraphs which follow. While it is impossible to identify all items which might need to be considered, the definitions and illustrations provided are examples of the decisions which must be made in planning for climate development and assessment.

1. DEFINE CLIMATE. In each setting and for each project, the meaning of the climate should be stated. The focus, the

Figure 1. Planning for Climate Development

Step or Task	Person(s) Responsible	Target Date for Completion
1. Define Climate		
2. Validate Climate Definition		
3. Identify Audiences		
4. Assess Climate Concerns		
5. Select Targets for Climate Review		
6. Plan Review Process		
7. Diagnose Existing Climate Conditions and Outcomes		
8. Identify Desired Changes		
9. Review Findings		
10. Select Target Projects for Climate Improvement		
11. Identify Audiences for Each Project		
12. Identify Related Environments for Each Target Project		
13. Identify Resource Needs		
14. Specify Desired Outcomes for Each Target Project		
15. Select Strategies To Be Used		
16. Establish Timelines for Each Target Project		
17. Review Expected and Possible Outcomes		

Step or Task	Person(s) Responsible	Target Date for Completion
18. Develop Communication Plans		
19. Develop Evaluation Plans		
20. Review Feasibility of Plans Made		
21. Revise, Affirm, and Implement Target Plans		
22. Monitor Implementation Processes for Formative Evaluation		

limitations, the intentions, and the assumptions which accompany the definition should also be clarified. Questions which can help might include:

- Is the emphasis to be upon the improvement of levels of satisfaction, levels of productivity, or both?
- Is the emphasis to be on processes selected to improve events or conditions or is it to be on outcomes which are expected as products within the environment?
- What is the audience being targeted for? What do different audiences expect as processes or products within the environment? How are judgments made about outcomes?

2. VALIDATE THE CLIMATE DEFINITION. The definition which is proposed—and the assumptions, limitations, and intended outcomes which are encompassed by that definition—should be validated. The major type of validation is acceptance by the audiences which experience or judge the environment in question. Is the definition understood by these audiences? Is the definition acceptable to these audiences?

3. IDENTIFY AUDIENCES. The audiences to be addressed will vary for each project planned. In a classroom, the major

audiences might include students, their parents, and administrators and colleagues of the teacher. For the school building or district, the target audiences might include students and employees, with attention being given to subgroups such as grade levels, departments, job classifications, and so forth. In addition, attention might be given to audiences at central office and to members of the board of education. Audiences external to the school include parents and patrons, prospective employers of graduates, institutions of higher education and similar groups.

4. ASSESS CLIMATE CONCERNS. Based on the definition selected and validated, the particular dimensions which define climate in a setting can be identified. These can be used as a basis for (a) organizing existing data about events, conditions, and outcomes and (b) identifying information which is needed to assess the current status. The dimensions of interest (dependent, in part, on the definition selected) are productivity and satisfaction. A survey which asks if the person is satisfied or dissatisfied, if the person sees the environment as purposeful and productive or not, and which also asks the person to identify desired changes is one method by which concerns can be identified. Charts of available data can also be used to identify concerns; for example, a chart of student attendance rates for the past five years, with comparisons to other schools in similar environments and to state or national norms for student attendance, can help to organize data to determine whether or not student attendance is a concern.

5. SELECT TARGETS FOR CLIMATE REVIEW. Based on the identified concerns, targets for review of climate should be selected. Whenever possible, the "Rule of 3s" should be followed; for example, identify the three major concerns of each audience, review these concerns, and determine the probability or lack of probability that efforts at change could lead to meaningful differences in climate outcomes. In this review process, awareness of the findings of research can be helpful. Some general guidelines include:

- If levels of satisfaction with the environment and its outcomes are at an 80 percent level or higher, it is unlikely that any project undertaken will have major noticeable and measurable effects on the climate which is present. If the levels of satisfaction are between 60 percent and 80 percent, efforts to improve conditions and outcomes are likely to be a wise use of resources. If the levels of satisfaction with the environment and its outcomes are less than 60 percent, climate improvement efforts are definitely indicated.

- When more than a single audience has a legitimate interest in the levels of satisfaction and productivity present in an environment, it is possible (and, at times, probable) that the priority of their concerns will vary. Actions which are planned and implemented for climate development should be acceptable to 80 percent or more of the persons in each audience. An alternative is to provide options, i.e., when multiple options are provided, there is a greater probability that all options will be perceived as desired or as acceptable for use with others by a larger number of the audiences and their members.

- The cliché claims variety is the spice of life. Too much variety, however, leads to confusion and usually results in lowered levels of satisfaction and productivity. Other problems may occur because of difficulties in the allocation and use of resources. As a general rule, planning for and providing three options is a recommendation to be followed as a means of maximizing efforts to provide for variety while avoiding chaos (Rule of 3s).

6. PLAN THE REVIEW PROCESS. When targets have been established, the process to review each target should be planned. Issues to be considered include:

- What are the sources of data which should be consulted?

- What data are already available as a part of the ongoing, record-keeping practices of the school?

- What are the practices for assessment which are known to the profession? What are the levels of appropriateness, reliability, validity, and usefulness of each?

- Are resources available to provide an adequate review process?
- Based on professional sources and knowledge, what are reasonable indicators and reasonable levels of attainment of satisfaction and productivity for the particular target? (Identifying expectations in advance of review can help to distinguish between "real" problems and dilemmas.)

7. DIAGNOSE EXISTING CLIMATE CONDITIONS AND OUTCOMES. Using the review process, diagnose the climate conditions and the outcomes being achieved. In many instances, attention will need to be given to both current data and data from previous years. To organize and interpret the data collected, criteria for interpretation should be established prior to collection of data. Illustrations of types of criteria which may be appropriate include:

- Comparisons of existing levels of satisfaction and productivity with levels attained in other classrooms or schools considered to be "comparable" to the environment being assessed.
- Comparisons of existing levels of satisfaction and productivity with levels attained with similar classroom groups or by the same school at earlier points in time.
- Comparisons of existing levels of satisfaction and productivity with (a) national or regional norms, (b) professional goals and ideals, or (c) evidence from research studies.

8. IDENTIFY DESIRED CHANGES. The data collected, when interpreted by consideration of criteria established in advance of collection, should permit the identification of answers to two basic questions: (a) Is it likely that efforts at change would be a wise use of resources because changes in outcomes are possible? (b) Can changes in outcomes be identified and can alternative plans for seeking changes be formulated?

A number of dangers are present at this stage of planning for climate development. One danger is that, as happens all too frequently, the preceding stages are not carried out and planning begins with uninformed brainstorming of "desired changes." A second danger is that a small group or a single person (perhaps the principal or an outsider to the school) will use personal power or prestige to advocate a particular problem and a particular solution. A third danger is that failure to carefully analyze and review existing conditions and outcomes will result in false identification of a problem. It is important that those who are involved in planning seek to provide proactive leadership, avoiding for self and for others reactive positions which respond to issues and events, or propose and advocate single solutions, without attention to long-range patterns and needs.

The four publications summarizing the Model Schools Project, conducted during the 1970s by the National Association of Secondary School Principals with support from the Danforth Foundation, provide ideas which can help planners to avoid these errors. (Trump, 1977; *NASSP Bulletin,* November, 1977; Georgiades, 1978; Trump and Georgiades, 1978.)

9. REVIEW FINDINGS. A review of the information collected and organized in the first eight steps should be completed before selecting specific targets for climate improvement projects. This process can be enhanced by outside help, such as practitioners and researchers who know climate development and assessment as well as colleagues from other schools who do not have a vested interest in the conditions and practices in the environment being studied. The use of outsiders will enable the identification of targets which are less likely to being chosen because they represent someone's pet project.

10. SELECT TARGET PROJECTS FOR CLIMATE IMPROVEMENT. The Rule of 3s can be useful in selecting targets for climate improvement. Simultaneous planning of climate improvement projects which are aimed at each primary audience (in a school, these audiences might be students, staff, and home-school relationships) can focus attention on one or more points of interest and concern for almost all persons who are involved in the internal and external environments

of the school. Assume that all projects to be planned have an ultimate goal to improve the levels of satisfaction and productivity attained by students. A number of projects might be identified as possible targets:

- A review of the testing program to be certain that standardized tests being used are compatible in content with the instruction being provided.

- A parent education project with concrete involvement of parents in understanding and support of classroom instructional practices.

- Development of multi-year profile sheets (or charts painted on the walls of the building) to illustrate how well the school has done and is doing in (a) student achievement scores as compared to student aptitude, (b) reduction of vandalism, (c) attendance, (d) self-esteem and other similar indicators.

- An inservice program for teachers which is based on the assumption that teachers can master a new skill and which teaches, by example, the attitude that most learners can master most learning objectives if provided with sufficient time on task and appropriate instruction.

11. IDENTIFY AUDIENCES FOR EACH TARGET PROJECT. Identify the audience which will experience the intervention as well as the related interventions which might need to be made. In addition, consider who needs to know about the planned interventions as well as who will want to know about the interventions and the results. For example, a project undertaken to improve attendance will require that parents and patrons, students, and staff understand and accept the goal and the strategies to be used. Also, if resources will be needed to carry out the project, central office personnel and members of the school board need to be informed and involved. Often, the communication plan which does or does not accompany a planned intervention is the actual key to its success or failure.

12. IDENTIFY RELATED ENVIRONMENTS FOR EACH TARGET PROJECT. Most climate development projects aim to effect

desired changes in outcomes experienced by a particular audience. The two most common audiences are students and staff. One of the assumptions here is that all projects have an ultimate target of improving the levels of productivity and satisfaction attained by students. A project aimed at student outcomes, however, will influence the environment of others; thus, staff may need to acquire new behaviors in order to implement new practices, or the active involvement of parents may be a requisite for success. Even if active involvement of staff or parents and patrons is not required, these audiences will need to be informed and involved in understanding and accepting the plans which are made. In identifying the related environments or audiences which will need to be considered, it is helpful to remember that:

- Any goal may or may not require expertise for implementation of intended activities, i.e., it will be an "expert" or "non-expert" task.

- Parents and patrons will tend to defer to educators if the task is perceived to be a function of role or expertise, for example, selection of instructional methodologies to be used.

- Students or parents and patrons are less likely to defer to educators when the task is perceived to be a "non-expert" task, for example, setting goals, determining appropriate disciplinary practices, selecting learning experiences desired by or seen as relevant to the student.

- Goals for climate improvement which are aimed at what students will experience or attain will require that, at a minimum, students, educators, and parents understand and accept the events and conditions directed toward goal attainment. The levels of understanding and acceptance present in the home environment may be more crucial to project success than any facet of the school environment. (Walberg, 1979.)

- Care should be taken in identification of the "home" environment. There are three major "home" environments which are interactive with the school environment and which are major influences on the outcomes to be attained by students. These are: (a) the socioeconomic home, (b) the emotive home, and (c) the cognitive home. Only the socioeconomic home can be defined by reference to the actual physical living arrangements of the student; the emotive home and the cognitive home may be in other settings such as the peer group or referent individuals external to both the school and "home."

13. IDENTIFY RESOURCE NEEDS. For projects which are planned, adequate resource support must be available so that plans can be implemented. Without such support, it is often better to do nothing than it is to create new expectations which cannot be fulfilled. Resources commonly needed include: (a) fiscal resources to cover added costs or costs of initiation of a project, (b) personnel resources with the motivation and skills to operate the proposed project, and (c) expert resource help (including either or both materials and consultative personnel).

14. SPECIFY DESIRED OUTCOMES FOR EACH TARGET PROJECT. Both process changes and product outcomes should be stated. Process changes include changes made in existing conditions or events. Product outcomes represent desired or intended changes in the outcomes to be attained. All too often, efforts are made to develop or improve the climate of a classroom or a school but the focus is limited to process changes without adequate attention to intended changes in product outcomes. In summative evaluations of climates which exist, however, it is product data that will be of greatest importance. Thus, to the greatest extent possible, the specification of desired changes should be expressed as changes in product data (outcomes) that are anticipated as a result of changes made in processes used within the environment.

15. SELECT STRATEGIES TO BE USED. The completion of earlier steps in this planning process usually will mean that, by this point, a number of possible strategies have been identified. Review these strategies. Consider their appropriateness for the setting in which they have been used. Consider their appropriateness for the setting in which they are being

considered for use. General criteria for review and selection of strategies for implementation include:

- Validity and legitimacy of practices for the setting in which they are to be introduced.
- Known product data about effectiveness in other settings.
- Feasibility of the practices for the setting in which they are to be applied (including attention to cost, to alternative strategies, and to the availability of expert help for implementation).

Perhaps the single most important recommendation to be followed in selecting strategies is to avoid hastily adopting a practice which worked in another setting. Every strategy should be viewed as a "tool," with value only insofar as it effects changes in product outcomes.

16. ESTABLISH TIMELINES FOR EACH TARGET PROJECT. A sequence of planned steps should be prepared for each project. Organize the timeline to show both direct tasks and enabling tasks—plans for inservice may be enabling tasks in a project aimed at improving student levels of satisfaction and productivity. The timeline should show a number of decision points when formative evaluation data is reviewed and decisions made about changes in the project.

The planned timeline for the project should be anticipatory; this goal can be met by planning a timeline which projects needed activities over a period of time having three cycles. In school settings, a "cycle" is usually a calendar or school year; in some instances, the cycle will be a semester, a period of time covered by a negotiated contract, or some other unit of time. The importance of planning for three cycles is another application of the Rule of 3s and is based on patterns which are known to be true in most social environments:

- During the first cycle of a change effort, novelty will keep energy and attention to project goals at high levels. This is the "honeymoon" or "Hawthorne" effect.
- During the second cycle, increased familiarity and skill with both the goals and the objectives will often result in

increased attainment of objectives. New concerns and new problems, however, will lead to questions about the project, including questions about whether it should be continued and whether it is legitimate.

- During the third cycle, processes of "culling" and "institutionalization" will occur. Much of the fanfare and folderol which may have accompanied the project will disappear and processes that do not work will be eliminated while practices or strategies which do work are maintained and begin to be seen as examples of "the way it's supposed to be" and "the way we have always done it."

Attention to timelines and to anticipated effects of the passage of time on both the appropriateness and efficiency of projects is a crucial part of the planning and decision-making process.

17. REVIEW EXPECTED AND POSSIBLE OUTCOMES. After strategies and timelines have been selected and established, the expected or anticipated outcomes of the project should be reviewed. Confirm and affirm the intended outcomes. Identify the product goals and outcomes that are being sought. Determine whether or not these goals are relatively permanent—will they remain as goals within the environment even if the processes used to attain goals are changed?

Evaluate practices being used or being considered for implementation to check for both intended and unintended outcomes. Has a particular practice raised the level of satisfaction? Has it also been accompanied by a decline in productivity? Have levels of productivity been raised at the expense of morale or satisfaction? Interaudience effects should also be considered; for example, has the introduction of a peer counseling program been successful in meeting the needs of students? Has it also led to lowered satisfaction with the work environment on the part of teachers? Has the introduction of a teacher-adviser system improved teacher-teacher and teacher-student communication but resulted in lessened home-school communication and involvement?

18. DEVELOP COMMUNICATION PLANS. Who needs to know? Who wants to know? Who has a right to know? How can these needs for information and communication be served most effectively and efficiently? The answers to these questions are the basis of the communication plan. It is not uncommon to observe settings in which internal communication about an existing or innovative practice is good to excellent while external communication is poor or non-existent. At times, the reverse is true but this is a less common condition. Strategies for communication should be selected as part of the process of developing the communication plan. Steps in developing the communication plan include:

- Identifying the audiences to be informed or involved.

- Determining the appropriateness of both formal and informal communication practices.

- Distinguishing between "expert" and "non-expert" tasks and areas of decision making.

- Determining the strategies which are to be implemented to be certain that opportunities are provided to individuals and groups for involvement in, and information about, the project.

19. DEVELOP EVALUATION PLANS. Plans for evaluation should provide for both formative and summative evaluation of the project, with consideration given to what intended as well as unintended outcomes occurred. Planning for evaluation, of course, is important, including how to obtain necessary resources for evaluation and how to communicate the results to appropriate audiences. The elements of the evaluation plan should include:

- Review of goals and objectives of the environment and the project.

- Review of the intended product outcomes (Step #14).

- Review of methods, procedures, and tools for possible use in data collection. Consideration should be given to cost, ease of administration, appropriateness of tools, known levels of validity and reliability, availability of expert help for data interpretation, and similar concerns.

- Provision whenever possible, for collection of data from multiple sources.

- Collection of "goal-free" information to determine whether or not unintended effects occur.

- Data interpretation and data storage and retrieval.

- A timeline for reporting project outcomes to appropriate audiences.

20. REVIEW FEASIBILITY OF ALL PLANS MADE. A review of all planning steps completed up to this point should be made. Use both internal and external personnel for this review. The purpose is to prune and refine. The plans for climate development must: be efficient and likely to be effective, represent wise use of resources, and be perceived to be legitimate by appropriate audiences.

21. REVISE, AFFIRM, AND IMPLEMENT TARGET PLANS. As a followup to the review of feasibility, efforts should be made to incorporate changes into the plans and to obtain confirmation and affirmation of the plan so that implementation can begin.

22. MONITOR IMPLEMENTATION PROCESSES FOR FORMATIVE EVALUATION. As described in early steps of this process, plans for formative evaluation should be made before implementation. As implementation occurs (in accordance with results that are observed and with results of data collected at planned intervals according to the timeline for the project) the project processes and outcomes should be reviewed so that decisions are made to improve the project, to continue or maintain the project, or to eliminate the project.

Summary

Careful planning for assessment of climate and for climate development projects is an imperative. Without careful planning, efforts are likely to be random, i.e., no matter how well-intended, the results have a 50 percent chance of being ineffectual, counterproductive, or lacking in satisfaction for all who are affected.

CHAPTER 4

Leadership for Climate Improvement

L eadership for climate improvement requires skills in responding to concerns, expectations, and existing conditions or initiating new expectations and conditions. The ultimate purpose is the improvement of learning.

The principal, more than any other individual, is responsible for a school's climate. The teacher has the same responsibility and accountability in the classroom. In either setting, effective leadership for climate improvement requires that they be:

- Aware of the conditions and events that influence personal attitudes, beliefs, and behaviors.

- Alert to the conditions and events that influence professional attitudes, beliefs, and behaviors.

- Aware of the expectations of others and know whether or not those expectations are understood.

- Aware of the responses to conditions or events that cannot be controlled but must be coped with.

- Able to plan, initiate, and implement events or changes that influence conditions which can be controlled.

- Able to formulate long-range plans for maintenance and improvement of conditions and events which influence the quality of outcomes attained by students.

Leaders for climate improvement must set high expectations for themselves as well as others. In a school building or in a classroom they have to establish expectations, design plans to permit self and others to reach expectations, and to recognize those conditions which either impede or enhance the realization of expectations.

Setting Expectations

Practices and conditions which prevail in schools and classrooms represent a mixture of traditions and beliefs which may or may not be supported by research. Two publications (Walberg, 1979; Lezotte, et al., 1980) contain a review of major research about what does and what does not influence the development of positive school and classroom climates. The findings reported in these two publications contradict many cherished, but unsupported, beliefs about education.

Brookover, et al. (1970) reported that the one factor which seems to explain most school-to-school and pupil-to-pupil differences in achievement is the "sense of futility." As described in Lezotte, et al. (1980), this sense of futility explains "more than 50 percent of the variance in achievement between schools. . . and is highly related to teacher expectations and student perceptions of those expectations." Lezotte and his co-authors suggest:

> An alternative to the bell-shaped normal curve is the J-curve of conforming behaviors, developed and tested by Allport (1934). The J-curve of conforming behavior suggests that most individuals can come to high level of mastery of a skill even without extraordinary interventions. Examples of this curve of conforming behavior would include learning to drive, to walk, or to talk. While these types of learned behaviors are commonplace, and are an important part of understanding how and why people think and act as they do, most educators have never heard of the J-curve of conforming behavior (even though nearly all have been "well-schooled" in the normal curve).

> Suppose that we began with the assumption that reading, writing, or arithmetic skills are not distributed in a bell-shaped fashion, but rather, these basic skills are more like walking, talking, and driving in that they are presumed to be learned like other J-shaped conforming behaviors. If this presumption were operating, decisions about curricular materials, instructional strategies, and assessment procedures would

clearly be different. Educators would quickly discard those patterns and practices that did not reinforce this belief and similarly, would retain those that did. The difference would be that in fairly quick fashion, the proportion of children that would learn to read would approximate the proportion of children that learn to walk or talk.

This perspective leads to the conclusion that "effective schools have a common belief that all students can learn, and they have adopted an instructional orientation that reflects this belief. . . one particular orientation—the concept of mastery learning—seems especially useful in promoting effective instructional programs."

There's an old story about a person who had a hobby of collecting the sayings which appear on bumper stickers. On one occasion, he was driving along a highway and, in front of him, a truck was pulling a horse trailer. On the back of the horse trailer was a bumper sticker which said: "What You See Is What You Are." The parallel is true for those who are responsible for exercising leadership for climate improvement; it is likely that what will occur will be closely related to what is expected. Unrealistic expectations, however, of self or others, will lead to a "sense of futility" and to a corresponding drop in both satisfaction and productivity.

Exercising Leadership

An assumption of this monograph, stated in the first chapter, is that learning is both a social and a psychological process. The implications of this for climate improvement are simple and clear. While it is important in exercising leadership for climate improvement to focus on the needs of the individual, changes are not likely to occur unless equal attention is given to changes in the beliefs, expectations, and norms of groups in both school and classroom settings. If we assume that schools or classrooms are sterile environments and that outside influences—socioeconomic status, home background, and others—totally impede efforts to achieve high levels of student satisfaction and productivity, it is likely that schools will become sterile environments. If we fail to understand the interaction of these influences on the expectations we have of youngsters or if we fail to understand the expectations held for children by agencies outside the school, we are also less likely to help students achieve desired levels of satisfaction and productivity in school-related endeavors and in life.

In a sociological sense, everyone has a role in life in which the position is either subordinate, equal, or superordinate. Most individuals focus their concerns and expectations at the levels which immediately surround them. Thus, in any position, the individual mediates between subordinates and superordinates.

The central office and the board of education serve a mediating function between the community or the broader society and the building administrator. The building administrator serves a mediating function between the expectations of the central office and the expectations of the staff. The classroom teacher is the mediator between the expectations of the supervisor or building administrator and students. Students, faced with school expectations as well as family, neighborhood, and social expectations need to mediate among these demands and respond in ways which permit social and psychological functioning.

When the ultimate criterion for assessment of the quality of school environments is the level of productivity and satisfaction attained by students, three areas of school climate development emerge as the focal points for improvement: (1) the climate experienced by faculty and thus transmitted to students, (2) the classroom climate experienced by students, and (3) the climate and interaction between school and family, neighborhood or social group environments. These areas of climate development are discussed later.

Responsible leadership for climate improvement rests on an understanding of a number of assumptions which were discussed in the first four chapters.

ASSUMPTION 1: Efforts at improving levels of satisfaction (morale) are not necessarily accompanied by increases in productivity or achievement.

In school environments, concerns about the levels of satisfaction and productivity for students and for staff are legitimate. Efforts to improve either the satisfaction or the productivity of students and staff are desirable. It is not wise, however, to assume that increases in the levels of satisfaction for staff will lead to increased staff productivity, increased student satisfaction or increased student achievement. Research findings are, for all practical purposes, unanimous in noting that the relationship between changes in staff morale and changes in other outcomes must be evaluated on a site-specific basis in each environment. Increases in staff or student morale can be accompanied by decreases, increases, or no change in other outcomes of interest.

ASSUMPTION 2: Increases in either productivity or satisfaction for one audience or group can result in decreases in levels of satisfaction or productivity for other groups.

Patterns of organization and staffing desired by teachers may have no effect, or negative effects, on levels of satisfaction or productivity as experienced or perceived by students and patrons.

ASSUMPTION 3: Environments have changing characteristics and changes in the population of major groups which "inhabit" the environment. Thus, a practice or condition which is appropriate at one time may be inappropriate or even counterproductive at a later time.

As knowledge, skill and understanding increase, people will desire differing opportunities for involvement in decision making, selection of alternatives, and rewards or recognition. Students, for example, are not satisfied or productive when asked to complete tasks that are merely repetitive of what has already been learned in school or nonschool environments. Parents and patrons do not appreciate not being involved in decision making concerning issues on which they feel qualified. An example is when conflict over discipline practices occurs between home and school. Teachers are unlikely to be satisfied with, or supportive of, practices which are maintained by tradition but which are unsatisfying and not reflective of classroom realities.

ASSUMPTION 4: Because environments differ from one another, and because the conditions in a single environment change over time, practices selected for use should not be assumed to be optimum until implemented and tested in the specific setting.

One illustration is how to best achieve a desired outcome of improving student skills in student-teacher, student-student, or student-parent communication. In some settings, a peer counseling program might be an effective approach. In still other settings, efforts which increased student contact and interaction with adults in multiple types of settings might be most effective. In other settings, establishment of a teacher-adviser program might be used to seek this outcome. Similar illustrations can be given for improving home-school communication. Formal reports are adequate in instances where the home is already familiar with school policies, practices, and behaviors and is supportive. In other instances, parent views which are negative about the school or low levels of parent understanding of school programs and practices may mean that methods of face-to-face and one-on-one communication are most appropriate. Similar examples are appropriate as a means of improving supervisor-supervisee relationships among administrators and staff.

ASSUMPTION 5: Interventions designed to change conditions within an environment and thus to change levels of either or both satisfaction and productivity will have intended and unintended effects. Therefore, all interventions should be planned and evaluated by examination of the results that occur as well as by examination of the results that are intended.

The importance of awareness and willingness to evaluate all effects that occur is crucial to making changes which can be institutionalized and which can become a part of the on-going pattern of the school environment. Have increases in satisfaction for a group been achieved with maintenance or improvement of productivity for the same group? Have increases in satisfaction or productivity for one group been achieved at the expense of lowered satisfaction or productivity for other groups? What priorities will be placed on decisions which must be made when values or expectations differ between different audiences? These questions should be carefully considered at all stages of planning, implementation, and institutionalization.

ASSUMPTION 6: Options within a setting, in contrast to uniform and monolithic practices, are more likely to produce maximum levels of both productivity and satisfaction when expectations are clear. Too many options, however, lead to confusion and to an increased probability of lowered levels of either or both satisfaction and productivity.

In plans for instruction, for classroom management, for home-school communication, for inservice and staff development, and a host of other illustrations, options should be provided. The teacher who can state expectations for classroom behaviors—both social and academic—and who can provide students with two or three options as to how those expectations can be met is likely to obtain higher levels of student satisfaction and achievement than in classrooms where options are not provided. The teacher who can choose from among a number of inservice or staff development activities, as contrasted to being required to participate in an activity required of all teachers, is more likely to be motivated and involved and is more likely to internalize some or all of the understanding and skill desired as an outcome of the activities selected. As a general rule, provision of three alternatives provides an optimum situation. Fewer alternatives leave the individual without a sense of choice and involvement; more alternatives often lead to feelings of confusion about what to select.

Impediments to Leadership

Efforts to exercise leadership for climate improvement in schools or classrooms sometimes run into a number of real or perceived impediments, mainly the kind that result from misunderstanding by those who will be affected. They frequently see the proposed changes as threats to their basic security or as being imposed without their involvement. The single greatest impediment to change, however, is inertia, often voiced in such statements as:

—It won't work.   —You don't understand our problem.
—We've tried that before.   —The new teacher won't understand.
—We've never done it that way.   —The experienced teachers won't use it.
—It's not good enough.   —We have too many projects now.
—There are better ways than that. —Can't someone else do it?

Four common forms of inertia or resistance to change are institutional traditions, the existing formal structure, group norms, and the habits of individuals (Lezotte, et al., 1980).

Pressures for change can overcome or modify the influence of these impediments. One of the most effective approaches is to increase the level of awareness of all audiences—students, patrons, and staff—so that pressure for change increases. A second way to increase the probability of change is to bring in new leadership—new administrators or new teachers. Mandates from outside sources such as funding foundations, guidelines of federal and state agencies, or decisions of legislative and judicial bodies often influence change.

Perhaps the most effective approach in fostering change, however, is to have those who will be responsible for new behaviors or those who are recipients of the new behaviors perceive the intended change as a means of improving their personal condition. Enlightened self-interest is a major motivator for change.

Summary

An individual's ability to be an effective leader for climate development is dependent upon the conditions one experiences and the conditions one creates. Setting expectations, exercising leadership, and understanding how to cope with and overcome impediments present in the setting are essential for effective leadership.

Mental and physical health, feelings that life and life's roles are both productive and satisfying, are key personal determiners of readiness for leadership. All people are influenced by their biochemical, physical, sociocultural, and psychological environments. An individual not satisfied with his or her personal life, i.e., relationships with significant others, cannot serve adequately as a leader for climate development. A person in poor health is also unable to serve as a leader for climate development. A third example of dissatisfaction with career choice or career role; in such instances, effectiveness as a leader is also reduced.

Awareness, optimism tempered by realism, and a "can do" attitude are essential to efforts to improve climate. Equally important is a sense of patience and a willingness to seek long-range, and often partial, solutions to complex problems.

CHAPTER 5

The Principal and Climate Leadership

In any human environment, people tend to be most concerned about the actions and behaviors of immediate superordinates and subordinates. From the moment that a principal is named, a number of groups and individuals will perceive this person as a superordinate. For students, teachers, other staff employees, parents, and patrons of the school attendance area, the principal has the role power and the role responsibility to make decisions which will influence their lives. Despite concern about the possible erosion of the principal's power, the principalship remains the single most powerful role in the American school by virtue of the degree of visibility accorded to it on the school campus and in the school attendance area.

The principal, on the one hand, may be authoritarian in forming and implementing decisions on the basis of role power; or authoritative in behavior, exercising leadership through application of expertise and motivation of others. On the other hand, the principal may be able to exercise leadership through personal charisma or prestige resulting from earlier successes.

Regardless of the principal's leadership behaviors, the principal is the individual in the school who is most responsible for the climate of the school and for the outcomes of productivity and satisfaction attained by students and staff.

41

The simple truth is that others respond, directly or indirectly, to what the principal does as well as to what he does not do.

Delegation of power, duties, or responsibility is possible and, indeed, necessary if the principal is to exercise leadership. Yet, in the eyes of many persons, the principal remains accountable for the climates that exist. Levels of satisfaction and productivity, actual and perceived, are seen as a direct or indirect result of what the principal has done. A few examples illustrate this point:

- Although the teacher establishes the climate within a particular classroom, students and their teachers remain convinced that the principal can and should reward "good" teachers and dismiss, correct, or replace "bad" teachers. Teachers also expect that the principal will notice, and act with regard to, teaching performance.

- In schools with strong department level organizations, or in schools where the principal has a number of assistant administrators, staff and students tend to view the principal as having a greater degree of power than other administrators or supervisors and believe that this power could be exercised if the principal chose to do so.

- When internal audiences—employees and students—are satisfied with the environments of the school and generally perceive these audiences as being productive in meeting their interests and needs, the principal is described as a "good" principal. If external audiences make the same judgment, the principal has job security or a springboard for career success.

Although the principal is the climate leader in most schools, exceptions exist. In small school districts, where there is one superintendent and one principal at each level, the superintendent probably serves as the climate leader for both the district and the school. In other instances, the effectiveness of the principal in fulfilling the role as climate leader is limited when cliques having both power and leadership exist. These cliques can include parents or parent groups as well as teachers who have reputations of expertise and prestige within the school or school-community.

The principal's role in climate leadership will vary in degree from setting to setting. At times, the principal will provide direct leadership. At other times, the principal will work through supervisors and administrators in the building or through faculty leaders. As a rule of thumb, however, faculty, students, parents, and patrons of the school will hold the principal accountable for all aspects of building operation unless a particular condition is viewed as being beyond the principal's authority. Application of the Rule of 3s to this expectation would suggest that the principal with three years or more in a building is likely to be held accountable for 60 percent or more of what is or is not occurring. The patterns that exist are those the principal has initiated or has permitted to exist.

The Climate Experienced by Principals

Principals, like other human beings, exist in a number of environments. In the personal dimension, the principal has expectations for self and is also the target of expectations from others, for example, home. In the job role, the principal has expectations for, and is the target of expectations from, a number of sources: (a) job superordinates, (b) job subordinates, (c) peers, (d) the profession, (e) the community, and (f) the larger society.

Expectations of the principal will be formed and modified according to the principal's own perception of constraints present in the role. Principals surveyed in the late 1970s by the National Association of Secondary School Principals (NASSP) reported that they perceived a number of constraints on the exercise of leadership. Their major concerns included:

- *Federal Regulations.* Student rights, Title IX, and provisions related to the use of categorical funds (Title I, special education, etc.) were major concerns.

- *State Requirements.* Regulations on compulsory attendance and regulations on the use of categorical funds were perceived as major constraints.

- *Central Office and School Board.* Limitations on job performance, as perceived by principals, included policy restrictions, lack of support, and interference in performance of job duties.

- *Community.* Problems in school-community relations, cited by principals, included lack of parent interest, parent demands, and pressures from special interest groups.
- *Within School (Students).* Three concerns about student performance or behaviors were the major concerns expressed by secondary principals: student absenteeism, student lack of motivation, and student discipline problems.
- *Within School (Faculty).* Three in every four principals surveyed perceived unprofessional behavior by teachers as a constraint on principal leadership and 84 percent reported variations in teacher ability as a roadblock to school success.

Expectations that the principal has for climate leadership by self as well as expectations held for the performance of others are formed not only by the principal's perceptions of existing constraints but also by the principal's beliefs about educational issues and about what is desirable in schools. Comparison of the results of surveys conducted in 1965 and in 1977 showed that in 1977 secondary principals experienced major shifts in what was perceived as being desirable. In 1977, as contrasted to 1965, principals were more likely to favor:

- Placing limitations upon classroom discussions of political "isms" and "anti-isms";
- Requiring more academic work of students;
- Justifying as practical each subject taught in the secondary school;
- Eliminating attendance requirements for students who are disinterested or hostile toward schooling;
- Changing the compulsory attendance rules and regulations to lower age levels;
- Providing specific job training for students;

- Providing special programs for educating the academically talented;
- Designing special programs for the handicapped, ethnic minorities, and non-English speaking students;
- Securing community support before undertaking major changes in school programs;
- Recognizing the need for legislation and court decisions which guarantee confidentiality of the records of students and staff;
- Providing for equal treatment of the sexes;
- Providing due process for protection of student rights.

Climate Concerns of Principals

In 1979, a random sample of principals who are members of NASSP were asked to rate the importance of climate relationships commonly experienced by students in schools (see Figure 2) and also to indicate the extent to which these relationships were being systematically studied in the building in which the principal worked (see Figure 3).

From the data shown, a number of inferences may be made. First, it is evident that secondary school principals place a strong emphasis on the importance of environmental conditions. Their attention is centered on (a) the emotional environment, (b) the social environment, (c) the sense of purpose present in the environment, and (d) the cognitive environment. Secondly, principals are interested in four major types of climate outcomes for students in school environments: (a) achievement, (b) development of self concept, (c) changes in behavior, and (d) changes in attitude. Lesser degrees of attention are given to the degree of structure present in the school environment or to physical conditions of the school environment. Principals do not place a high priority on the development of social relationships among students as an outcome of the school environment.

Despite the levels of interest and concern shown for environmental conditions and outcomes, Figure 3 shows that principals do not believe climate relationships are systematically studied. Also, that data are not being used as a basis for planning, decision making, and selecting intervention strategies to bring about changes in the climate conditions and outcomes. Systematic studies of these relationships are conducted, on the average, less than 20 percent of the time.

Figure 2. Ratings by Secondary School Principals of the Importance of Specific Climate Relationships for Student Populations

Internal and External Conditions of School Climate	Mean Scores Condition: Outcome Relationships					
	Achievement	Self Concept	Behavior Changes	Attitude Changes	Social Relationships	Row Mean Score
Emotional Environment	2.86	2.88	2.79	2.76	2.54	2.76
Social Environment	2.24	2.69	2.52	2.53	2.72	2.54
Sense of Purpose (Goals)	2.71	2.52	2.49	2.52	2.14	2.48
Cognitive Environment	2.63	2.43	2.26	2.33	2.10	2.35
Structure	2.34	2.09	2.24	2.07	1.97	2.14
Physical Environment	2.15	1.94	2.04	1.94	1.73	1.96
Column Mean Scores	2.49	2.43	2.39	2.36	2.20	2.37

Mean scores shown in Figure 4 are based on a rating scale defined as follows:

3 = High Importance
2 = Moderate Importance
1 = Low Importance
0 = Not Important

Figure 3. Rank Order of Specific Climate Relationships and Percentages of the Extent to Which These Relationships Are Measured as Reported by Secondary School Principals

Rank Order	Environment: Outcome Relationships	Mean Score of Importance	Relationship Is Measured in Schools (%)
1	Emotional Environment: Self-Concept	2.88	20%
2	Emotional Environment: Achievement	2.86	21%
3	Emotional Environment: Behavior Changes	2.79	26%
4	Emotional Environment: Attitude	2.76	26%
5	Social Environment: Social Relationships	2.72	19%
6	Sense of Purpose: Achievement	2.71	24%
7	Social Environment: Self-Concept	2.69	14%
8	Cognitive Environment: Achievement	2.63	46%
9	Emotional Environment: Social Relationships	2.54	18%
10	Social Environment: Attitude Changes	2.53	18%
12	Social Environment: Behavior Changes	2.52	20%
12	Sense of Purpose: Attitude Changes	2.52	18%

Rank Order	Environment: Outcome Relationships	Mean Score of Importance	Relationship Is Measured in Schools (%)
12	Sense of Purpose: Self-Concept	2.52	15%
14	Sense of Purpose: Behavior Changes	2.49	16%
15	Cognitive Environment: Self-Concept	2.43	21%
16	Structure: Achievement	2.34	21%
17	Cognitive Environment: Attitude Changes	2.33	26%
18	Cognitive Environment: Behavior Changes	2.26	18%
20	Social Environment: Achievement	2.24	14%
20	Structure: Behavior Changes	2.24	12%
21	Physical Environment: Achievement	2.15	18%
22	Sense of Purpose: Social Relationships	2.14	12%
23	Cognitive Environment: Social Relationships	2.10	14%
24	Structure: Self-Concept	2.09	12%
25	Structure: Attitude Changes	2.07	17%
26	Physical Environment: Behavior Changes	2.04	16%

Rank Order	Environment: Outcome Relationships	Mean Score of Importance	Relationship Is Measured in Schools (%)
27	Structure: Social Relationships	1.97	13%
28	Physical Environment: Self-Concept	1.94	13%
29	Physical Environment: Attitude Changes	1.94	12%
30	Physical Environment: Social Relationships	1.73	13%

Examination of the information presented in Figures 2 and 3 leads to the conclusion that meaningful changes in climate conditions and climate outcomes are not likely to occur until principals exercise leadership for more systematic processes of assessing and developing the climate of schools.

Strategies for Improvement

A general hypothesis about how actions of the principal will influence levels of student productivity and satisfaction—the ultimate aim of efforts to improve school climate—is that the flow of effects is from the principal to teachers, from teachers to students, and from students to student outcomes (Walberg, 1980). More simply, the principal must rely on indirect acts which are transmitted and mediated by the faculty of the building.

Given this hypothesis that principal-initiated behaviors must have their primary impact on teachers' perceptions, intentions, and behaviors, the crucial tasks of the principal in exercising leadership for climate improvement include:

- Stating expected outcomes.
- Stating expected behaviors on the part of teachers as a means of achieving intended outcomes.

49

- Determining whether or not teachers understand and share in the expectations that have been established.

- Securing necessary support services so that teachers are able to implement behaviors aimed at accomplishment of expectations.

- Supervising teacher performance of expected behaviors.

- Providing feedback about teacher behaviors and about progress toward attainment of expectations.

- Collecting feedback from teachers (and, as appropriate, from other audiences) to determine the extent to which goals are being attained and the extent to which principal behaviors are helpful to, and supportive of, teachers in efforts at accomplishment of intended behaviors and intended outcomes.

To illustrate, assume that the climate improvement project is aimed to improve student discipline. The first step is to state expected outcomes; examples might include change in:

- The number of disciplinary referrals made by teachers to counselors and administrators.

- The number of referrals made by the school to other agencies when the problem is more appropriately served by other community agencies.

- Parent and patron perceptions of the quality and nature of discipline in the school.

- Student perceptions of the extent to which they are able to, or willing to, exercise self-discipline.

- Student perceptions of the extent to which discipline rules, regulations, and practices are illustrative of ways in which the school "teaches" good citizenship.

- The extent and nature of parent involvement in planning and selecting responses to disciplinary problems.

- The extent to which student, teacher and parent audiences perceive discipline to be one of the major problems in the school environment.

- Attendance of students or staff during the school day and at school activities as concern about discipline conditions declines.
- Academic performance of students as a concurrent outcome of declines in frequency of, or concerns about, disciplinary conditions.

Part of the process of stating intended outcomes should include: collecting and organizing data to reflect the pattern that has existed for the past three to five years; determining through surveys or other methods of data collection, the existing levels of concern and the expectations that are held by differing groups; and deciding the basis of comparision to be used to report progress toward goal attainment, e.g., comparison to previous years in the same school, comparison to data for other schools in the same school district or to similar schools in other communities, or comparison to state or national norms.

The second step is to identify those teaching behaviors that enhance the attainment of expected outcomes. Development of the behaviors considered appropriate in reaching some or all of the intended outcomes can permit teachers to select those that contribute to the overall goal of improving disci pline. Depending upon teacher competence, these activities might be aimed at levels of awareness, understanding, or application. In some instances, the behavior may be mandated; in others, it may be recommended; and, in still other instances, it may be suggested as an approach.

Having a variety of options available for teacher performance and growth is likely to increase teacher commitment to the task. It also provides for differences in knowledge or skill that exist within the staff as well as a foundation from which to build differing types of expertise among staff members to enable them to serve as resources to each other.

Mandated behaviors will include those that are already part of the school's rules and regulations, for example, requirements for reporting incidents of misbehavior by students, requirements for staff supervision of student behavior in classroom and non-classroom settings. Recommended strategies for teachers include:

- Developing and applying a plan for classroom management (described in Chapter VI).

- Developing awareness of, and utilizing, non-school agencies for referral of students.

- Developing, for any disciplinary incident, a minimum of three recommended solutions.

- Involving parents in establishing consequences for treatment of disciplinary infractions.

- Assessing student awareness of the teacher's rules, regulations and expectations in classroom and activity settings.

The remaining steps flow from the first two. The principal, in collaboration with the staff and with an understanding of parent and student expectations, should determine whether or not the staff understands and accepts both the goals and the strategies that are planned. In like fashion, the principal should identify the staff's expectations regarding the behavior of the principal and should clearly indicate which expectations are considered valid and which are contradictory to the principal's expectations. Plans for securing necessary support as well as plans for collecting and reporting feedback to both individuals and to the members of the school-community should be formulated. Planning steps described earlier could be followed to achieve these tasks.

Summary

The crucial task of the principal in exercising leadership for climate improvement is to establish and communicate expectations for long-range improvement. In this process, the principal must avoid pessimism on the one hand and "faddism" or unwarranted enthusiasm for a particular method or tool on the other.

In exercising leadership for climate improvement, the principal's major role is to provide the staff with the information, the expectations, the support, and the supervision so that the staff is able to serve as mediators and transmitters of the principal's expectations. If the principal's words or actions express either a sense of complacency or a sense of futility, this is the message the faculty will receive, respond to, and transmit. If the principal is both optimistic and systematic in messages which are transmitted, the staff will also be optimistic and thorough in performance.

Many principals do not realize the extent of the power they exercise and the mediating influence, for good or for bad, which their words and actions have on their faculties. When the principal does not trust the faculty, then the faculty does not trust the principal, one another, students, or parents. When the principal is laissez-faire in supervision of the faculty, the faculty is less committed to either social or academic behavior standards for students. When principals exhibit a siege mentality—with fear of parents, students, teachers, or all of these groups—teachers mirror the same behaviors.

Effective principals, and effective leaders for climate development, must see their role as both vocation and avocation. If there is a single tool which the principal should have, it is a mirror. Looking in that mirror, the principal can find the person who, more than any other, is both responsible for and accountable for, the feelings of satisfaction and productivity for staff, students, and patrons. The direct quality of the principal's leadership of staff leads to the mediated and indirect influence which the principal has on the climate experienced or perceived by students and patrons.

CHAPTER 6

How To Improve Classroom Climate

T here are three kinds of people: those who watch what happens, those who make things happen, and those who say, "What happened?" Examples of teachers can be found in any of these categories. As Jacques Barzun once noted: "No limit can be set to the power of a teacher, but this is equally true in the other direction: No career can so nearly approach zero in its effect."

Thousands of books and articles have been written to describe what teaching is, what a good teacher is, and how teachers can be most effective or most efficient. While the findings and recommendations in these sources are important, they cannot all be reviewed or examined here. The task of describing the role of the teacher as a leader for climate improvement in the classroom, however, is not a difficult one.

Effective Teachers

Throughout history, both professional and commercial literature has illustrated the characteristics of effective and ineffective teachers. Most visitors to a classroom can quickly conclude that some teachers are more effective than others. Effective teachers can be found in schools having weak leadership and certainly in those having strong and effective leadership. In schools experiencing conflict, some teachers provide classroom environments that are not only safe and secure but are also characterized by good student-student and student-teacher relationships as well as by a sense of purpose and achievement (Kelley, 1970).

While the quality of the total school environment will influence the climate of a particular classroom, the presence of effective and efficient classroom environments in both good and bad school environments leads to a single conclusion: teachers are accountable for the climate in their own classrooms. Effective teachers accept this accountability. In addition, effective teachers are more likely to exhibit the following characteristics and beliefs:

- Believes that the education of learners is important.
- Has high goals and standards for personal and professional performance.
- Believes that all, or almost all, students can learn and want to learn.
- Has high expectations for student performance, both social and academic.
- Exhibits personal security in relationships with students, peers, patrons, and superordinates.
- Selects instructional content and method with awareness and understanding of present levels of student performance and experience as well as student aspirations.
- Exhibits warmth, enthusiasm, a sense of purpose and a sense of humor in relationships with students.
- Has a reward system which is known to students and which permits distinction between correct and incorrect social and academic responses.
- Expresses a philosophy which aims at student mastery of expected behaviors and teacher use of time is flexible and supportive of this philosophy.
- Understands and plans for learning experiences on both social and psychological levels, i.e., practices indicate that the teacher understands each individual as an indi-

vidual and also as a member of a number of social roles or as an actor in a number of social environments.

- Distinguishes between single events and patterns of behavior, anticipates interactions with students rather than reacting to student behaviors.

In addition to personal beliefs and characteristics, the effective teacher must have knowledge and skills suitable for the tasks which are to be performed. Knowing how to organize and deliver instruction as well as evaluate both student performance and instructional effectiveness is necessary. Knowledge of content, and the ability to articulate the relevance of that content to the past, present, and future life orientations of the student is important. While the teacher will spend much time on "telling" students about content, attention should be given to "selling" students on content, i.e., showing students how the content being studied relates to their environment and their experiences or aspirations. To do so with effectiveness requires that the teacher be familiar with the other environments the student experiences as well as the aspirations which the student holds as life goals.

Classroom Organization and Management

Effectiveness in the classroom requires that the teacher's plans for organization and management begin with the expectation that students can and will learn appropriate social and academic behaviors.

Although most teachers are skilled in planning their instruction, some teachers experience failure. This can occur when student interest is not developed prior to instruction, when students have a sense of complacency because teacher expectations are too low, or when students experience a sense of futility because they are asked to complete tasks beyond their readiness and preparation.

In contrast to instruction for mastery of content, many teachers fail to give adequate attention to planning for classroom management practices and for instruction related to appropriate classroom behaviors. One solution to this problem is the development of a "lesson plan" for classroom management (Kelley, 1978). A number of steps are appropriate in the design of such a plan:

- Existing school policies, rules, and regulations should be reviewed by the teacher as a basis of planning for classroom rules and instruction related to those rules.

- Rules and regulations should be formulated for expectations in the classroom. To the greatest extent possible, students should be involved, perhaps in brainstorming activities, in stating expectations and setting rules and regulations.

- Rules and regulations, once formulated, should be reviewed by the teacher with input from other teachers and from supervisory personnel. A final draft of classroom rules and regulations should be prepared.

- Copies of the classroom rules and regulations should be printed and distributed to students, parents, and to appropriate supervisory personnel.

- A copy of the rules and regulations should be posted in the classroom in a location where it is visible and available for review by both students and the teacher.

- One or more instructional lessons should be planned to provide students with opportunities to understand and learn the rules and regulations of the classroom. Lessons in classroom management can be used at the beginning of each quarter or semester of the school year and should be used whenever there are major shifts in the population of the classroom group. Instruction in classroom rules might include study of appropriate sections of the student handbook of the school, study of the rules and regulations established for the classroom, study of parallel examples in the society and in work environments, and discussion of the relationship between classroom, building, and district rules and regulations.

- Instruction about classroom management practices should include information about the procedures the teacher will follow in application of the rules and regulations. In addition, the teacher should specify positive student behaviors which are desired and which will be rewarded within the classroom. Instructional activities might include brainstorming activities as a means of obtaining student input into the formation of rules and regulations as well as simulations of appropriate and inappropriate classroom behaviors. Group discussions of student expectations of one another and of the teacher can also be a vital part of instruction.

- Instruction for classroom management should follow the same principles which applied to planning instruction for subject matter content. Involvement of students in brainstorming expectations for student and teacher behavior is a means of motivating students, providing for ownership, and establishing classroom norms. Periodic review, perhaps every three or four weeks, provides opportunities for reinforcement, clarification, and praise for appropriate behaviors. In such a review session, the teacher can focus upon positive behaviors, areas of concern, and necessary revision or clarification of classroom rules, regulations, and procedures.

In planning for classroom management, as is true for all other types of planning, plans for evaluation should be made early. Some examples of appropriate evaluation tools and procedures might include: (a) surveys of students to identify their level of understanding and acceptance of classroom rules and procedures, (b) recording of behaviors to identify the patterns of behavior which reflect attainment of expected classroom behaviors, (c) surveys of parents to identify their understanding, acceptance, and endorsement of classroom rules and regulations, and (d) collection and analysis of attitudinal data which indicate whether or not students find the teacher's behaviors to be both reasonable and fair. Use of these data can help in planning for revision of practices used; such a review, with appropriate revision, is recommended on an annual basis.

Self-confidence. The development of rules and regulations for classroom management, and planning instruction related to those rules and regulations, is unlikely to be effective if the teacher is not comfortable with the student population, the teaching assignment, and the philosophy which is normative for the building. Teachers must be able to project a sense of purpose and self-confidence in their relationships with students.

Sense of Timing. Problems in classroom management are, more often than not, attributable to poor timing of teacher responses. Effective classroom management requires established norms and teacher skill in diagnosing and responding to events which occur. Teachers should seek to have the "punishment fit the crime," and this means that consequences of behavior should be assigned with the same care that is given to planning for individual needs in other areas of the curriculum. The application of predetermined consequences, without diagnosis, is less effective than careful diagnosis of the consequences which are appropriate given both the event and the pattern of behavior shown by the student (*NASSP Bulletin,* September, 1978). A common aspect of poor timing is over-reaction to minor events rather than planning for, and responding to, patterns of behavior shown by individuals and groups.

In addition to teacher *self-confidence* and a *sense of timing*, effective classroom management requires teacher openness to student feedback, teacher willingness to model democratic behaviors, and a sense of fairness. Fairness, for example, is not shown in the routine application of discipline strategies without consideration of how those strategies match with the learner's needs and characteristics (*NASSP Bulletin,* September, 1978).

Suggestions

Numerous strategies and practices are available for teachers to maintain or improve classroom climate. In most instances, care should be taken to diagnose the environment before planning major changes: "If it ain't broke, don't fix it!" Some practices which are almost always appropriate include:

- Develop skills in, and use, a variety of teaching methods.
- Provide alternatives in resource materials which can be used by students for preparation of assigned work.

- Study the use of time to be certain that time spent on task is congruent with the importance of the task.

- Review the class list on a regular basis (perhaps once a week) to monitor the nature and type of communication you are having with students.

- Check student understanding and awareness of the teacher expectations for social and academic behaviors.

- Inform parents and whenever possible involve them in classroom activities.

- Communicate with the home and with persons significant to learners about their accomplishments and suggest out-of-school strategies for reinforcement of classroom experiences.

- Become aware of the interests of students; show interest in their out-of-classroom and out-of-school experiences.

- Brainstorm the major outcomes—attitudinal, academic, and behavioral—which you expect and plan methods of assessment so that instructional effectiveness is assessed.

Summary

Every classroom group is also a special group. The teacher's role is to ensure that every effort is made to cause things to happen, to foster formation of a positive academic and social environment within the classroom group. Practices of good communication between home and school as well as articulation to other parts of the school program are essential for effective classroom climate. Strategies that seek to involve the home, students within the classroom, and other parts of the school program are usually effective in improving classroom climate or in making a good classroom climate even better.

The teacher's expectations of self and expectations of students provide the starting point for positive classroom climate. As is true in all aspects of climate development, the goal is to avoid a sense of futility or sense of complacency on the part of students. Instead, the goal is to stimulate "creative tension," a condition in which there is a gap between what the student knows and can do, accompanied by realistic expectations by the student that the gap can be narrowed or closed.

CHAPTER 7

Improving the Climate of Home-School Relationships

An ancient Chinese proverb states that "One parent is worth a thousand teachers." While the ratio may not be a thousand to one, a growing body of research supports the conclusion that the home may be the single most important factor in determining how much and how well a learner learns (Walberg, 1979; ASCD, 1979; Lezotte, et al., 1980). Efforts at increasing the extent to which the home is involved in, concerned about, and understands the learning experiences provided in the school are likely to have a greater impact on student academic and social behaviors than are many of the efforts of educators to improve school and class-room climate.

Educators, in statements of belief more than in practice, have recognized the importance of the home. The reverse, unfortunately, is also true. All too often, educators have offered as a rationalization for social or academic behaviors the comment: "Well, what can you expect? He comes from a poor home background!"

The home and the school are partners in establishing the "climate" of expectations that a youngster must confront.

Either or both environments can contribute to a sense of complacency. Either or both environments can contribute to a sense of futility. Either or both environments can contribute to the development of a sense of expectancy, purpose, and pleasure for the learner.

While the existence of research-based relationships between socio-economic status (SES) and achievement are well documented, the sense of hopelessness expressed by many educators about whether or not schools can have an effect on student achievement and behaviors is unwarranted (Lezotte, et al., 1980). As Ira Gordon noted (ASCD, 1979), three sets of family factors are associated with development. In addition to SES, which is not subject to meaningful intervention by schools, the cognitive set within the family and the emotional factors that characterize the family are important. Schools can plan programs to increase parent (and patron) awareness of the programs of the school; in like fashion, schools can plan strategies to help parents improve the richness of the cognitive environment provided within the family as well as strategies to help parents improve the emotional environment of the family.

Given the importance of parents in the education of their children and given the research findings on "time on task," one expects that home-school communication would receive more attention, more time, and more resources than more traditional areas of concern such as: (a) selecting and improving instructional materials, (b) revising and establishing school-based rules for conduct, and (c) sessions at schools and professional conferences which lament the lack of involvement by the home in the education of children.

The perspective of educators about home-school relationships should be reflected in the practices which are selected and implemented. The strategies suggested here reflect the following assumptions:

- At all levels of schooling, high levels of parent involvement should be a goal.
- Parent involvement is most effective when parents view their participation as directly linked to their child's opportunity to meet the expectations of the school.

64

- Parent and community involvement is a legitimate activity of schools and an integral part of its delivery of services.

- Educators should be committed to involvement of parents and patrons in the education of children.

Improving Community Involvement

Schools belong to their publics. Parents and patrons should be involved in such tasks as setting goals, reviewing instructional materials, assisting with classroom and non-classroom activities offered by schools, determining information needs of parents and patrons, reviewing the adequacy of information provided by testing programs and by practices used to report pupil performance and behavior. As suggested in Chapter 6, parents should be informed about and involved in the review of classroom rules and regulations.

Practices should be developed to provide inservice opportunities for teachers and parents to develop additional skills in enriching the cognitive environment present in the home. Parent-teacher-child conferencing that is directed toward goal-setting rather than toward reporting of past performance is one appropriate strategy. A second strategy is to provide a list of home-based activities which will support instruction to be offered during the next few weeks or month. Working with parents and patrons to identify community resources available to the home and the school can be a positive experience; such a resource list can identify individuals who are able to contribute to classroom activities and can increase the extent to which adults, other than employees, are present in school settings. The added involvement of parents usually has a positive impact on student behavior, student attention to task, and adult understanding and approval of the school and its performance.

Existing practices of home-school and school-community communication should be reviewed and, if appropriate, revised. All too often, practices of communication are too routinized and too bureaucratic. A common error is the failure of professional educators to distinguish between "expert" and "non-expert" tasks. Selection of instructional methods, for example, is usually considered to be an "expert" task. Selection of discipline practices, however, is a non-expert task; indeed, often, the home may be more aware of practices which are effective in promoting desired behaviors than is true for the school or teacher.

Special efforts should be made to involve patrons who reside in the attendance area of the school in school activities. Many persons, if asked, are willing to become involved in, and contribute to, school programs.

Consideration should be given to identifying the information about the school which parents and patrons want to know or, in the eyes of the school, should know. Preparation of "fact sheets," planning neighborhood gatherings, or conducting a survey of "adult awareness" can help to transmit a realistic picture of the school and can also serve to enlist adult support for needed changes.

Communication between the home and the school, or between community members and the school, should be planned with attention to the level of understanding which parents or patrons have about the school or about tasks which they are asked to become involved in. The more "removed" an adult from the school environment, the more important it is that communications be personal and face-to-face rather than formal and bureaucratic in tone. Setting up personal relationships between an employee of the school and the families served in the neighborhood can foster a continuing pattern of home-school communication.

Other suggestions helpful to teachers and principals in working with parents and patrons include:

- Monthly newsletters from teachers to review what has been covered in class, outline future class activities, and suggest questions or comments or activities which parents can use to discuss their child's classroom experiences.

- Sending collections of written work prepared by the student home and asking for parent feedback about the work, e.g., a set of compositions prepared in an English class, a set of laboratory exercises completed in a science class, or tapes of work completed in-class in foreign language or in drama.

- Use of audiotaped reports which are mailed or sent home with the child and which provide parents with an opportunity to send a taped message back.

- Developing a year-long plan to have a small number of parents present at weekly intervals as visitors and contributors to classroom activities. Suggested ways of involvement and pre-planning for involvement are essential to success.

- Developing assignments for students which instruct them to confer with parent or other adults in reviewing the assignment.

- Developing a list of questions commonly asked by parents at parent-teacher conferences and mailing this list in advance as a means of having parents determine the topics they would like to have covered in the conference (as contrasted to the more common practice of teacher-dominated conference techniques).

- Developing a schedule for home visitations to be made by the classroom teacher or other school personnel—school planning for such a practice might utilize a "family counselor" approach and designate a faculty member for each family served by the school.

Summary

Efforts to improve the climate of a school or a classroom must be understood by, and acceptable to, all the audiences which will be influenced by what happens. Active involvement of parents and patrons can increase the levels of effectiveness and efficiency as well as the levels of satisfaction which are experienced by staff and students in schools and classrooms.

Positive leadership for increased and improved home-school communication should be provided by the building administrator. It is usually this administrator who must plan for the coordination of efforts at increasing home-school and community-school relationships since these relationships will require support in time, use of space, and use of other resources. In addition, active and positive encouragement of staff to increase levels of external communications will be necessary in most instances.

CHAPTER 8

Summary Thoughts

S herlock Holmes turned to Watson and said: "And, then there is the strange matter of the barking dog." "But," Watson replied, "there was no barking dog." "Precisely," said Holmes, "and that is what I find so strange."

An observer of American education during the past quarter century might find it strange that few concentrated efforts by practitioners and researchers have been undertaken to determine the relationship between satisfaction and productivity in schools. After all, there is general agreement that school environments should be both productive and satisfying for those who are influenced by these environments.

A number of efforts have been aimed at improving the feelings of satisfaction experienced by educators, students, and parents or patrons. There has also been a multitude of efforts aimed at improving the levels of achievement attained by students or the levels of productivity shown by educators and by schools as organizations. Often, these efforts have been undertaken with the assumption that improvement in one dimension will be accompanied by improvement in the other, i.e., increases in satisfaction or morale will be accompanied by increases in productivity or achievement. Research findings, however, do not confirm predictability of this assumption. Both may increase, but it is equally (or even more) probable that one will increase and the other will decrease or that both will decline.

High levels of productivity and satisfaction are goals for outcomes to be sought for all persons who work and study in school environments. If priorities must be set, however, the ultimate criterion is the level of productivity and satisfaction attained by students. The welfare of students must be the overriding concern of parents, patrons, and educators.

In *A School for Everyone*, J. Lloyd Trump states a theme which is echoed in this monograph: "Schools can be better than they are. The programs that conventional schools provide today serve some individuals reasonably well; other persons need quite different arrangements." (That text, and others which describe the Model Schools Project—an eight-year project sponsored by the Danforth Foundation and conducted by the National Association of Secondary School Principals between 1968 and 1976—reflect concerns similar to those discussed in this monograph.)

While strategies have been used to illustrate approaches that have worked in some school environments, the emphasis in this text is on the diagnosis of school, classroom, and home or community environments as a basis for planning and implementing climate improvement projects. Such projects should be carefully monitored and evaluated; and educators need to subscribe to a code of professional accountability which supports the use of legitimate processes as well as holds that the legitimacy of processes is not sufficient unless the product outcomes, measured in terms of human satisfaction and human productivity, warrant their continued use.

The improvement of school and classroom climates, and the improvement of the conditions which foster desired climate outcomes, ultimately depends upon the willingness of educators to seek a state of "creative tension," i.e., a commitment to the belief that schools can be better and a willingness to test approaches to improve school environments. At the same time, educators need to oppose a "sense of complacency" or a "sense of futility" in both self and others.

Selected References

Association for Supervision and Curriculum Development. *Partners: Parents and Schools* (Alexandria, Virginia: ASCD, 1979).

Brookover, W., Beady, C., Flood, P., Schweitzer, J., and Wisenbaker, J. *School Social Systems and Student Achievement: Schools Can Make A Difference* (New York: Praeger Publishers, 1979).

Brookover, W.B. and Lezotte, L.W. *Changes in School Characteristics Coincident With Changes in Student Achievement* (East Lansing, Michigan: College of Urban Development, Michigan State University, 1977).

Consulting Psychologists Press. *Diagnostic Tests and Teaching Materials*, 1979 Catalog (Palo Alto, California: Consulting Psychologists Press, 1979).

Epstein, Joyce L. and James M. McPartland, "The Concept and Measurement of the Quality of School Life," *American Educational Research Journal*, Winter, 1976, 13:1, 15-30.

Epstein, Joyce L. and James M. McPartland. *The Quality of School Life Scale and Technical Manual* (Boston: Houghton Mifflin, 1978).

ERIC Clearinghouse on Educational Management. *Research Action Brief*, "School Climate," February, 1978, Number 4.

Ewald, William R., Jr., editor. *Environment for Man: The Next Fifty Years* (Bloomington, Indiana: Indiana University Press, 1967).

Fox, Robert S., et al. *School Climate Improvement: A Challenge to the School Administrator* (Bloomington, Indiana: Phi Delta Kappa, Inc., 1973).

Georgiades, William. *How Good Is Your School?* (Reston, Virginia: National Association of Secondary School Principals, 1978).

Howell, Bruce and Bill Grahlman. *School Climate: Evaluation and Implementation*. (Tulsa, Oklahoma: CADRE Publications Center, College of Education, University of Tulsa, undated).

Kelley, Edgar A. "Case Studies and An Analysis of the Role of Morale, Organizational Climate, and Conflict in the Study of Secondary School Environments" (Doctoral dissertation, Michigan State University, 1970).

Kelley, Edgar A. *How You Can Measure Teacher Perceptions of School Climate* (Dayton, Ohio: Institute for the Development of Educational Activities, Inc., April, 1974).

Kelley, Edgar A. "Developing a Lesson Plan for Classroom Discipline," *Action in Teacher Education*, 1:2, 41-45.

Lezotte, Lawrence W., et al. *School Learning Climate and Student Achievement* (Tallahassee, Florida: SSTA Center, Teacher Education Projects, Florida State University, 1980).

Madaus, G.F., et al. "The Sensitivity of Measures of School Effectiveness," *Harvard Educational Review*, 1979, 49:2, 207-230.

Moos, Rudolf. *The Social Climate Scales: An Overview* (Palo Alto, California: Consulting Psychologists Press, 1974).

Moos, Rudolf. "A Typology of Junior High and High School Classrooms," *American Educational Research Journal*, 15, 53-66.

Murray, Henry A. *Explorations in Personality* (New York: Oxford University Press, 1938).

National Association of Secondary School Principals, *NASSP Bulletin*, November, 1977 (Entire issue is a review of the Model Schools Project).

National Association of Secondary School Principals. *The Senior High Principalship: The National Survey.* Volume 1 (Reston, Virginia: NASSP, 1978).

National Institute of Education. *High School '77: A Survey of Public Secondary School Principals* (Washington, D.C.: U.S. Department of Health, Education and Welfare, The National Institute of Education, 1978).

Owens, Robert G. *Organizational Behavior in Schools* (Englewood Cliffs, New Jersey: Prentice-Hall, Inc., 1970).

Rutter, Michael, et al. "Fifteen Thousand Hours: Secondary Schools and Their Effects on Children," *The New Republic*, June 16, 1979, 31-34.

Searle, Herbert A. "Professional Secrets," *NASSP Bulletin*, September, 1979, 88-92.

Stern, George. *People in Context* (New York: John Wiley and Sons, 1970).

Trump, J. Lloyd. *A School for Everyone* (Reston, Virginia: National Association of Secondary School Principals, 1977).

Trump, J. Lloyd and William Georgiades. *How To Change Your School* (Reston, Virginia: National Association of Secondary School Principals, 1978).

Walberg, Herbert J., editor. *Educational Environments and Effects: Evaluation, Policy, and Productivity* (Berkeley, California: McCutchan Publishing Company, 1979).